016

ANCIENT GREECE

JANE SHUTER

Heinemann

www.heinemann.co.uk/library

Visit our website to find out more information about **Heinemann Library** books.

To order:
 Phone 44 (0) 1865 888066
 Send a fax to 44 (0) 1865 314091
🖥 Visit the Heinemann Bookshop at www.heinemann.co.uk/library to browse our catalogue and order online.

First published in Great Britain by Heinemann Library, Halley Court, Jordan Hill, Oxford OX2 8EJ, part of Harcourt Education. Heinemann is a registered trademark of Harcourt Education Ltd.

Editorial: Jilly Attwood, Kathy Peltan and Vicki Yates
Design: David Poole and Tokay Interactive Ltd
Picture Research: Hannah Taylor
Production: Camilla Smith

Originated by Chroma Graphics (Overseas) Pte. Ltd
Printed in China by WKT Company Limited

ISBN 0 431 07905 6 (hardback)
10 09 08 07 06
10 9 8 7 6 5 4 3 2 1

ISBN 0 431 07911 0 (paperback)
10 09 08 07 06
10 9 8 7 6 5 4 3 2 1

British Library Cataloguing in Publication Data
Shuter, Jane
Ancient Greece
938
A full catalogue record for this book is available from the British Library.

Acknowledgements
The publishers would like to thank the following for permission to reproduce photographs:
AKG Images pp. **14** (Andrea Baguzzi), **19**, **22** (Erich Lessing), **26** (Nimatallah), p. **11**; Alamy Images p. **17** (Stephen Bond); Ancient Art & Architecture Collection pp. **6**, **7**, **15b** (Ronald Sheridan), **10** (Mike Andrews) **21** (J. Kline), pp. **8**, **28**; Corbis pp. **4** (Third Eye Images), **12** (Gianni Dagli Orti), **16** (Michael Nicholson), **18** (Erich Schlegel), **25b** (Adam Woolfitt), **27** (Araldo de Luca); Getty Images pp. **9** (Photodisc), **29** (Stu Forster); Harcourt Education Ltd pp. **15t** (Fiona Freund), **24l**, **24r** (Richard Butcher & Magnet Harlequin); The Art Archive p. **13** (Dagli Orti); Werner Forman Archive p. **25t**.

Cover photograph of the Parthenon, Athens, reproduced with permission of Corbis Royalty Free.

The author would like to thank Robyn Hardyman, Bob Rees and Caroline Landon for their assistance in the preparation of this book.

Any words appearing in the text in bold, **like this**, are explained in the glossary.

Contents

Exploring further

Throughout the book you will find links to the Heinemann Explore CD-ROM and website at www.heinemannexplore.co.uk. Follow the links to discover more about a topic.

What do the symbols mean?

The following symbols are used throughout the book:

 Source

 Word detective

 Biography

 See for yourself

Where and when was ancient Greece?

The ancient Greek **civilization** lasted from about 800 BC to 146 BC. Ancient Greece was not a single country, but was made up of many small **city states**. All Greeks spoke the same language and worshipped the same gods.

City states

The first Greeks chose a place that was good for farming and lived there in small groups. These groups traded and fought with each other. Soon, the small groups began to join together into city states. Each city state was made up of a city and the land and villages surrounding it. The best cities were built on hills with walls around them. A city high up on a hill was called an **acropolis**. If the city state was attacked, all the people of the city crammed into the acropolis for safety.

Working together?

Some city states had just a few hundred **citizens**. Others had thousands of people. Big city states were the most powerful and tried to control their weaker neighbours. Although city states fought each other, when enemies who were not from Greece attacked, they joined together to fight back.

The landscape of Greece affected how it developed as a country. The mountains and the sea made travel dangerous. They also made it difficult to form a single, unified country.

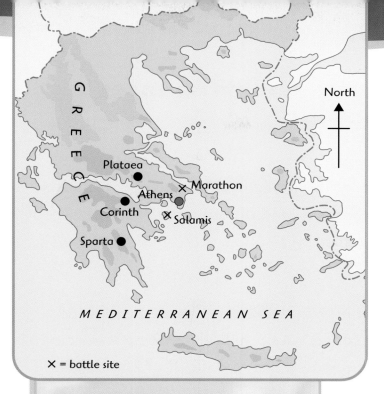

Athens, Sparta, and Corinth were the main city states in ancient Greece.

Exploring further

Use the Heinemann Explore CD-ROM or visit the website to discover more about life in ancient Greece. As well as text on all the key topics, you can explore pictures, biographies, written sources, and lots of activities. Go to the Contents screen. Click on the blue words in the list and off you go!

Aristotle was an important **philosopher** in ancient Athens. He wrote about the importance of having a city state that was neither too big, nor too small.

You can't have a city state of ten citizens. But when you have 100,000 citizens it is no longer a city state. It has to be big enough to run itself, but it has to be small enough for the citizens to know each other. Otherwise how can they choose officials?

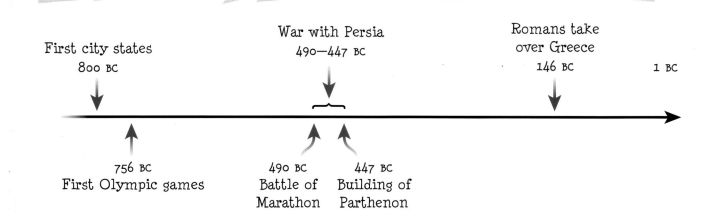

First city states
800 BC

War with Persia
490—447 BC

Romans take over Greece
146 BC

1 BC

756 BC
First Olympic games

490 BC
Battle of Marathon

447 BC
Building of Parthenon begun

What were the similarities and differences between Athens and Sparta?

The most powerful **city states** in ancient Greece were Athens and Sparta. Athenians and Spartans spoke the same language and worshipped the same gods, but they had separate rulers and laws, and different ideas on how their societies should be run. Athens and Sparta were also rivals.

Government

At first Athens and Sparta were ruled by kings. Then they were both ruled by small groups of powerful people called oligarchies. Later Athens became a **democracy**. This meant that Athens was run by a council of 500 officials who were voted for by the people. All laws were passed by an **assembly**, which met four times a month. Sparta remained an oligarchy, run by a group of warriors called the Spartiates.

Although democracy means 'rule by the people', only **citizens** could vote. Women, slaves, foreigners, and anyone aged under eighteen could not become a citizen. So democracy in Athens actually meant rule by the men of Athens.

This sculpture is from ancient Athens. The standing figure is 'Democracy'. She is crowning a man. The man represents 'the people' of Athens.

Word detective

The word 'democracy' means 'rule by the people'. It comes from two ancient Greek words: *demos* meaning people and *kratia* meaning rule.

Attitudes to outsiders

Athenians traded with other city states, and with countries outside Greece, such as Egypt. In contrast, the Spartans had very little to do with other city states and the outside world.

Evidence from Athens

We know more about Athens than about Sparta because there is more evidence from Athens. Athenians believed in education. They wrote down their ideas in plays, poetry, and books of all kinds. They also spent the money they made from trading on beautiful public buildings. Evidence of the books and the buildings has survived. Spartans did not value education in the same way and did not write things down. Their buildings were simpler than the Athenians and have not survived.

The Athenians traded beautiful painted vases like this one, which shows farmers picking olives. They also traded olives and olive oil. They traded these things for grain.

Plato

Plato (about 475–347 BC) was an Athenian writer, teacher, and **philosopher**. As a young man he was taught by another great philosopher, Socrates. Plato wrote about how city states should be ruled, and whether it is possible to teach people to behave well. In 386 BC Plato set up the first school for teaching philosophy and educating the future leaders of Athens. It was the first university and was called the Academy.

Exploring further

Use the CD-ROM or go to the website to find out:

- what the Athenians did to prevent an official from becoming too powerful
- how Athenians voted in the assembly
- who were the different groups of people in Sparta.

Try looking in 'Everyday Life' and 'Digging Deeper'.

Family life

Athenians and Spartans had very different views on family life. In Athens, the family was important. In Sparta, army life was more important than family life. In Athens, women ran the home, looked after the children, and did not go out of the house much. Most families also had **slaves** to help them. Men had to keep fit in case they needed to fight. In Sparta, both men and women were expected to exercise and keep fit. The men had to be able to fight, and the women had to produce strong and healthy children.

The writer Plutarch described the Spartans' attitude to babies and children.

The father brought the newborn baby to be examined by the leaders of the group. If they thought it was strong and healthy they let it live. If it was weak or deformed it was taken to an open place and left to die. Children were expected to eat whatever they were given, or not eat at all. Children were not allowed night lights; they were expected not to be afraid of the dark.

This Spartan statue shows a girl running. Spartan women exercised in public to keep healthy. Small statues like this one have been found by **archaeologists**. They can tell us a lot about daily life in ancient Greece.

City life

Athens was a busy city, with lots of beautiful buildings, shops, and public baths. Most people lived in simple houses, but rich people had nicer homes that were beautifully decorated. Rich men often had parties with lots of wine and food. Women were not invited to these parties.

The public buildings in Athens were very impressive. On the **Acropolis** the Athenians built the **Parthenon** and other temples. You can still visit the Acropolis today and see the remains of the buildings.

Most of the buildings in Sparta were made from mud bricks, or wood, only the temples were made from stone. Spartans ate simple food and did not drink much wine. They thought things that made life comfortable would make their warriors soft.

In about 414 BC Aristophanes, a Greek writer, described the bustle of a morning in Athens.

When the cock crows at dawn, up they all jump and rush off to work, the bronzesmiths, the potters, the tanners, the shoemakers, the bath attendants, the corn merchants, the lyremakers, the shieldmakers. Some of them even put on their sandals and go when it is still dark.

Exploring further

Compare the advantages and disadvantages of living in Athens or Sparta. Use the activities on the Heinemann Explore CD-ROM or visit the website. Look in 'Activities'.

What made ancient Greek fighters so powerful?

The ancient Greeks were very tough fighters. They fought off two big Persian invasions, even though the Persian army was far bigger than theirs. Why did this happen?

Practice on land and at sea

Greek **city states** often fought each other. They made sure that their men were always ready to fight. They also looked after their weapons and **armour**. All the men of a city state fought in the army. Their homes and families were at risk if they lost a battle. Greeks who lived on islands or on the coast were also good sailors. They knew the sea around their homes very well. This was useful in sea battles. Athens had a navy to protect all of Greece. Other city states helped to pay for this.

Greek warships were called **triremes**; this is a life-size copy. They were rowed by up to 170 men, and so were very fast. In a battle they would **ram** the enemy's ships. The Greek navy won a great victory over the Persians at the battle of Salamis in 480 BC.

Style of fighting

The ancient Greeks were very good at fighting. Most Greek soldiers were **hoplites** who fought on foot with spears and swords. They often fought side by side with their shields overlapping to make a wall. This is called a **phalanx** pattern. Each phalanx was about six men deep. If hoplites in the front row were killed, others stepped forward to take their places. The Greeks would choose a good place to use their phalanx and then wait for the enemy to attack.

These hoplites are putting on armour made from several layers of stiffened linen cloth. This was lighter, cooler, and cheaper than metal armour. The soldiers' helmets were made of metal and their shields were made of wood.

Exploring further

Look on the Explore CD-ROM or visit the website to find out more about:

- what **archaeologists** have found on ancient Greek battlefield sites
- how doctors treated Greek soldiers wounded in battle.

Look in 'Digging Deeper'.

Was the battle of Marathon a great victory for the ancient Greeks?

In 490 BC, a Persian army of about 200,000 soldiers landed on the coast near Athens. Athens and the nearby **city state** of Plataea only had 10,000 soldiers, so the Athenians asked Sparta for help. The Spartans said they would come after a big religious festival, but by the time they got there, the battle was over.

What happened at the battle of Marathon?

The Athenians and Persians were at either end of the plain of Marathon. The Persians had many more soldiers than the Greeks. At first, the Persians broke through the Greeks in the middle of their line of attack. But then, the Greek soldiers broke through at both sides of the Persian army and attacked them from behind. The Persians ran away. About 6400 Persians were killed, and only 192 Greeks died.

This painting of a Persian **archer** is on a temple wall. Neither the archers nor the horsemen were much use to the Persians at the battle of Marathon.

Was Marathon a great victory?

The Greek victory at Marathon stopped the Persian invasion of Greece. Even though there were many more Persians than Greeks, the Greeks won. Also, the Greeks only lost a few men. Although Marathon was a great victory for the Greeks, there was one bad thing that came from the battle. City states had always helped each other in wars against outside enemies. The Athenians lost trust in Sparta. People in Athens felt the Spartans used their festival as an excuse not to help.

Word detective

Today, a marathon is a race of about 42 kilometres (just over 26 miles). Some people believe that this comes from the fact that this was the distance that a runner travelled from Marathon to Athens, to tell the Athenians about the victory over the Persians.

Exploring further

Look on the Explore CD-ROM or visit the website to find out about:

- King Darius of Persia. Look in 'Written Sources'.

- The Battle of Thermopylae in 480 BC. Look in 'Exploring'.

- Pheidippides' run to Athens. Look in 'Exploring'

The ashes of the Athenian soldiers who died at Marathon were all buried together. This modern monument marks where they were buried.

13

Who did the ancient Greeks worship and why?

The ancient Greeks believed in many different gods and goddesses. They believed the twelve most important gods lived on Mount Olympus. They thought the gods were like a family who looked after each other, but also argued a lot.

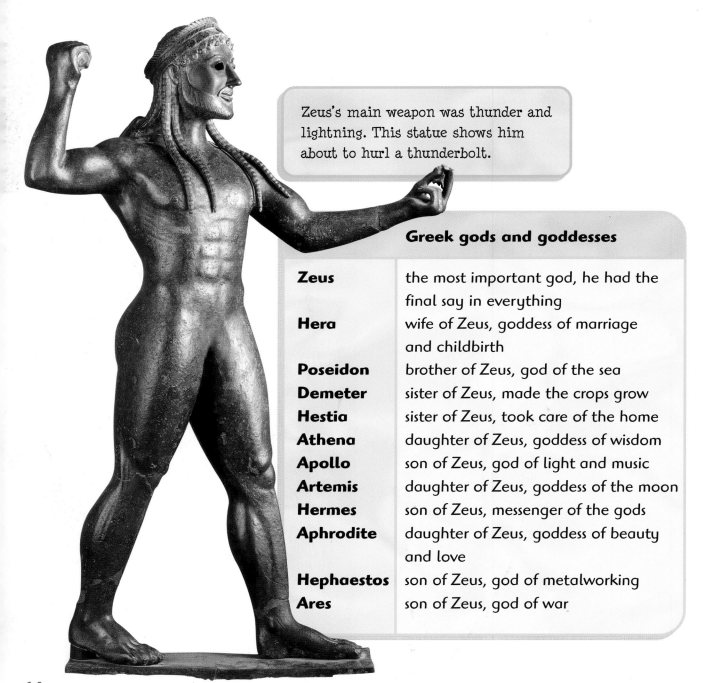

Zeus's main weapon was thunder and lightning. This statue shows him about to hurl a thunderbolt.

Greek gods and goddesses

Zeus	the most important god, he had the final say in everything
Hera	wife of Zeus, goddess of marriage and childbirth
Poseidon	brother of Zeus, god of the sea
Demeter	sister of Zeus, made the crops grow
Hestia	sister of Zeus, took care of the home
Athena	daughter of Zeus, goddess of wisdom
Apollo	son of Zeus, god of light and music
Artemis	daughter of Zeus, goddess of the moon
Hermes	son of Zeus, messenger of the gods
Aphrodite	daughter of Zeus, goddess of beauty and love
Hephaestos	son of Zeus, god of metalworking
Ares	son of Zeus, god of war

Keeping gods and goddesses happy

The ancient Greeks believed their gods and goddesses could change life on Earth. It was important to make the gods happy, then they would help you. Unhappy gods punished you. There were many special places where people could pray to the gods or leave them presents.

The Greeks built temples for their gods. They believed the work they put into the temple and the time they spent worshipping would please the gods. Big **religious festivals** outside temples could last for several days. They included sports and theatre shows.

Temples were homes for the statues of gods, not places for people to pray in. **Priests** looked after the statues. This is the Erechtheum, a temple on the **Acropolis** in Athens. It was named after Erechtheus, a legendary hero who was the first king of Athens.

See For Yourself

The British Museum, London

You can see some of the decorations from the Parthenon at the British Museum in London. The Parthenon is a temple to the goddess Athena, built on the Acropolis in Athens. A band of magnificent sculptures ran all the way round the top of the temple's inner building. They were brought to England in the early 19th century. They show scenes from a procession during a religious festival called the Panathenaic festival. They would originally have been painted in bright colours.

15

What happened at the theatre?

Almost every Greek city had a theatre. Plays were part of many **religious festivals**. In every theatre, there was an **altar**. The main acting space was used for **sacrifices**.

What did the theatre look like?

Greek theatres were open air and circular in shape. Most of the stage and **orchestra** was surrounded by seats.

Word detective

Scenery was an important part of plays. It was hung on a wooden framework called a *skene*. This where our word 'scenery' comes from.

This is the theatre of Dionysus in Athens. It was built below the walls of the **Acropolis**. The temple of Dionysus was just behind the stage. Plays were part of the religious festival of Dionysus.

What were plays like?

Plays were either spoken or sung in rhyme. The chorus was a group of fifteen people who told the story and made comments about what was happening in the play. The actors were always men. They spoke the big speeches for the main characters. Only three actors could be on stage at one time. They changed characters by putting on masks. The masks used a series of set faces to show young and old, male and female. Sometimes a mask had a happy side and a sad side to show what the character was feeling.

Tragedies and comedies

Plays could either be tragedies or comedies. Tragedies were stories about the gods. Things usually turned out unhappily. Two writers of tragedies were Sophocles and Euripides. Comedies were funny and had everyday storylines. They could also be quite rude.

See for yourself

The Minack Theatre, Cornwall

The design of modern theatres is still based on the Greek model, with curved rows of seats rising up from the stage. Most theatres in this style in Britain are indoors. But you can get a real taste of what an ancient Greek theatre might have been like by visiting this open-air theatre at Minack in Cornwall.

What do sources tell us about the importance of the Olympics to the ancient Greeks?

The ancient Greek Olympic games were part of a **religious festival** held to honour the gods. They were held every four years at Olympia. **City states** would agree not to fight each other for a month before and after the games. This allowed people to travel safely to and from Olympia, either to watch or to compete in the games. There are many different sources that can tell us about the ancient Greek Olympics.

Source 1

These people are watching the shot-put competition during the 2004 Olympic Games in Athens. This event took place on the site of the original stadium at Olympia, which you can see was much smaller than a modern Olympic stadium.

Source 2

Pausanias was a Greek writer and traveller in about AD 150. He wrote this description of an event that formed part of the Olympics called the **pankration**, which was like boxing and wrestling.

Arrachion's opponent held him with his legs in a powerful scissor grip. At the same time, he started to strangle Arrachion who, with the last of his strength, reached out and broke one of his opponent's toes. Arrachion died of the strangling. But, at the same time, the strangler gave in, because of the pain in his toe. So Arrachion was proclaimed the winner and crowned with the olive garland.

Source 3

The men in this ancient Greek vase painting are wrestling. We can learn a lot from Athenian pottery. Skilled artists painted in black on the reddish pottery. They liked to paint scenes from everyday life, as well as scenes from stories of the time about gods, goddesses and heroes.

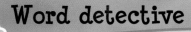

Word detective

Our word 'stadium' comes from the ancient Greek word *stadion*. A *stadion* was a measure of length. It was the length of the track used for running races at the Olympics. One *stadion* is about 185 metres (about 600 feet).

Source 4

The programme of events at Olympia:

- *Day One*
  sacrifices, oaths, checking of athletes

- *Day Two*
  morning: horse racing and chariot racing

  afternoon: pentathlon

- *Day Three*
  morning: religious ceremonies

  afternoon: boys' events

- *Day Four*
  morning: track events

  afternoon: wrestling, boxing, pankration, racing in **armour**

- *Day Five*
  banquets and **sacrifices**

How have the ancient Greeks influenced our language?

Greek is one of the languages that English is based on. Many of the words we use, especially words to do with education, maths, and science, come from Greek words. Often when a new word is needed for an invention or discovery, it is made up from Greek words.

One Greek word that we use is 'alphabet', from *alpha* and *beta*. These are the first two letters of the Greek alphabet.

The Greek alphabet

Capital	Lower-case	Greek name	English
A	α	Alpha	a
B	β	Beta	b
Γ	γ	Gamma	g
Δ	δ	Delta	d
E	ε	Epsilon	e
Z	ζ	Zeta	z
H	η	Eta	e
Θ	θ	Theta	th
I	ι	Iota	i
K	κ	Kappa	k
Λ	λ	Lambda	l
M	μ	Mu	m
N	ν	Nu	n
Ξ	ξ	Xi	x
O	ο	Omnicron	o
Π	π	Pi	p
P	ρ	Rho	r
Σ	σ	Sigma	s
T	τ	Tau	t
Y	υ	Upsilon	u
Φ	φ	Phi	ph
X	χ	Chi	ch
Ψ	ψ	Psi	ps
Ω	ω	Omega	o

You can see Greek writing on this coin showing Zeus on a throne with an eagle.

Look for the 'Word detective' boxes on other pages of this book. Here are some more examples of words we use that have come from Greek words.

Word detective

History is from the Greek for enquiry.

Technology and anything else starting with 'tech-' (e.g. technique) is from the Greek for a craft or skill.

Technology and anything else ending in '-ology' (e.g. archaeology) is from the Greek for 'to talk about a subject'.

Grammar is from the Greek word gramma, which means 'a letter of the alphabet'.

Geography and anything else starting with 'geo-' (e.g. geology) is from the Greek for 'of the Earth'.

Geography and anything else ending with '-graphy' (e.g. photography) is from the Greek for 'the science of'.

Photograph and anything else starting with 'photo-' (e.g. photosynthesis) is from the Greek for 'light'.

Photograph and anything else ending with '-graph' (e.g. autograph) is from the Greek for 'written down, recorded'.

Exploring further

Find as many words as you can that come from ancient Greek words. Use a dictionary of word origins to help you, and the Heinemann Explore CD-ROM or website. Look in 'Exploring, Change and Influences'.

What similarities are there between ancient Greek schools and our schools?

In ancient Greece, children in different **city states** were educated in different ways. Education was also different for boys and girls. Boys were taught to be good **citizens**. Girls were taught how to look after the house and family. Today, boys and girls are educated together and taught the same subjects.

What did children learn?

In some city states, like Sparta, reading and writing were not thought important. Boys left home at the age of seven to train for war. They might also learn their father's **trade**. In Athens, boys were taught how to make speeches. This was so they could help with running the city state. They also learnt different sports. They had to be fit to fight in the army.

In this vase painting of a lesson, a boy is learning to play an instrument called the lyre.

School

Between the ages of seven and fourteen, Athenian boys went to school each morning. There they learnt to read and write and did maths. They worked in small groups in one room. They read aloud and learned poetry by heart. Many pupils would have been able to recite the whole of Homer's great works, the *The Iliad* and *The Odyssey*. In the afternoon, they went to wrestling school where they learned sports.

At fourteen, the sons of tradesmen began to learn their trade. The sons of rich Athenians went to the **assembly**, the market place, and the **gymnasium**. Here they learned from the men how to join in **debates**, vote, and become fit and strong.

Equipment

Boys had stools, but no desks. They learnt things by heart instead of writing them down. If they needed to, they wrote on wooden boards covered with a layer of wax. They used a wooden pen, called a stylus, with a sharp end for writing and a flat end for rubbing out.

Homer

Homer lived sometime between 850 and 750 BC. He is said to have been the poet who wrote *The Iliad* and *The Odyssey*, two very important, very long poems about the Trojan wars. Homer lived very early in Greek history, so little is known about his life. He wrote powerful stories about brave, strong Greeks who behaved honourably. The Greeks loved them.

Exploring further

Use the Heinemann Explore CD-ROM or go to the website to find out more about:

- what the Greek thinker Plato wrote about Athenian education. Look in 'Exploring, Written Sources'.

- the Greek legends told by Homer in his poems. Look in 'Exploring, Everyday Life'.

How have the ancient Greeks influenced our buildings?

The ancient Greeks wanted their buildings, especially the temples, to be beautiful. They saw a beautiful building as one that was balanced and even. The Georgians and Victorians liked this balanced building style and copied it for many of their buildings.

Columns

Ancient Greek **architects** made buildings with lots of **columns** under a flat roof. A sloping roof could then be built on top of the flat one to carry away rainwater. Columns were made by stacking drum shapes on top of each other.

Building tricks

The Greeks used tricks to make their buildings look perfect. The columns are narrower at the top than at the bottom. If they just get slowly narrower, our eyes see a dip, about two-thirds of the way up. The ancient Greeks made their columns bulge a bit just at that point, to make them look perfectly smooth. For the same reasons, they made the floor a bit higher in the centre of the building and made the columns lean inwards slightly.

Columns were decorated in different styles. Doric columns (*right*) sit directly on the floor of the temple and have a plain **capital** (top). The capitals and bases of Ionic columns (*far right*) were more elaborate. The columns themselves were slimmer too.

This photo of the **Parthenon** shows how the ancient Greeks used maths to make their buildings look right. The height of the columns (**A**) is four-ninths the width of the Parthenon (**B**). This is called the Golden Rectangle. The width of each column (**C**) is also four-ninths the distance between them (**D**).

See for yourself

The British Museum, London

Many more recent buildings copy the building styles of the ancient Greeks. This is the British Museum in London. It was built in Victorian times, in 1852. This building looks a lot like the Parthenon, which you can see above.

Exploring further

Use the Heinemann Explore CD-ROM or visit the website to find out in detail how the architect and builders of the Parthenon made it one of the most beautiful buildings in the world. Look in 'Digging Deeper'.

What did ancient Greek thinkers tell us about history, geography, and other subjects?

The ancient Greeks thought it was important to find out about the world and how it worked, and to record what they found. They also thought it was important to think things through, and argue points well. They worked out many ideas that are still used today. Here are some of them.

History

The ancient Greeks were the first people to want to record the past as accurately and fairly as possible.

Geography and science

Eratosthenes was a scholar who worked out how big the Earth is. There was no way he could tell whether he was right or not, but other Greeks were pretty sure his ideas were right. Today, we know that he was only 67 kilometres (42 miles) out!

Heraclides was a thinker who made one of the first maps of the sky. He put the planets in their correct order from Earth.

Herodotus

Herodotus was a historian. He was the first person to suggest that it is important to write the facts when recording historical events. Herodotus always tried to be fair to all sides when he described wars or arguments. Unlike earlier writers, he did not automatically take the side of the Greeks.

Health

The ancient Greeks believed that to be healthy, a person had to take the right kind of exercise, eat the right foods, and get enough sleep. They also thought it was important for people to keep clean.

This sculpture shows a Greek doctor examining a patient. The ancient Greeks' ideas on medicine had a big influence on modern medicine. They began to record patients' symptoms, and to treat patients by watching them carefully and thinking about the illnesses they might have.

Hippocrates

Hippocrates has been called the 'father of modern medicine'. He collected together the writings of many Greek doctors. His name is given to the oath that all new doctors had to take until well into the 20th century – the Hippocratic Oath.

Maths

Pythagoras worked on **geometry**. He was especially interested in angles. We still use his ideas in maths today. Archimedes and Euclid were also mathematicians. Euclid collected together and wrote down all the mathematical ideas of the time.

How are the modern Olympic games like the ancient ones?

The ancient Olympic games were held every four years. When they were started up again in 1896, the new games were like the old ones in some ways, but there were also many differences.

When were the Olympics held?

The ancient Greek Olympics were held every four years, just like our modern ones. They were always held at Olympia, and lasted for only five days. They were part of a **religious festival** dedicated to the god Zeus. Only Greeks took part in the games. Today the Olympics are a big sporting event for countries all over the world. Different countries take it in turns to host them. The modern games last for just over two weeks.

This copy of an ancient Greek statue is of a discus thrower. Field events like discus and javelin throwing are still an important part of the Olympics today.

Who competed and what events were there?

At the ancient Olympics only men competed. They competed as individuals, not in teams. Today both men and women compete.

Both the modern and ancient Olympics included events that involved running, throwing, and jumping. However, in the modern Olympics there are new events such as cycling, shooting and swimming.

Winning at the Olympics

Athletes who won at the ancient Olympics got glory and a crown of olive leaves. Modern athletes get glory, and a gold, silver, or bronze medal.

Just like today, at the ancient Olympics one of the most popular sports was running. The Greeks raced against each other on sand to make it more difficult. As in modern athletics, there were different lengths of race. This 10,000 metre men's race was at the 2004 Olympics, which were held in Athens for the first time since the games were revived there in 1896.

Exploring further

Use the Heinemann Explore CD-ROM or go to the website to find out about:

- who could watch the ancient Olympics, and where they sat. Look in 'Exploring, Change and Influences'.

- what it meant for an athlete to win 'without dust'. Look in 'Written sources'.

- Milo, an ancient Greek Olympic hero. Look in 'Written Sources'.

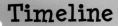

Timeline

800 BC	First **city states** are set up
700 BC	Homer is writing *The Iliad* and *The Odyssey*
735 BC	City of Rome, in Italy, is set up
776 BC	First Olympic Games
600 BC	Greek city states have over 1500 **colonies** around the Mediterranean
530 BC	Pythagoras is writing about mathematical ideas
490 BC	Persians invade. Battle of Marathon
480 BC	Persians invade. Battles of Thermopylae and Salamis
450 BC	Athens is at the height of its power
447 BC	Building of the Parthenon begins
440 BC	Herodotus is writing his histories
400 BC	Sparta is at the height of its power
400 BC	Plato begins writing about perfect governments
336 BC	Alexander the Great becomes king of Macedonia
334 BC	Alexander the Great invades Persia and proceeds to conquer a great empire
323 BC	Alexander the Great dies
310 BC	Romans begin to conquer an empire
146 BC	Romans take over Greece

See for yourself

British Museum, London
Wonderful collection of works of art from ancient Greece, including sculptures from the Parthenon and vases, as well as objects from everyday life.

Lady Lever Art Gallery, Liverpool
Large collection of painted vases from ancient Greece.

Royal Museum, Edinburgh
Displays some ancient Greek painted vases.

City of Manchester Stadium, Manchester
Visit to get a sense of how the ancient Greek Olympics have influenced our sports events today. The stadium was built to host the Commonwealth Games in 2002.

Glossary

acropolis hilltop fortress in ancient Greece

altar table in a temple

archaeologist person who digs up and studies things left from past times

archer soldier who fights with a bow and arrow

architect person who designs and constructs buildings

armour covering for particular parts of the body used to protect solders in battle

assembly in Athens, this was where all the citizens gathered together to vote on laws or actions

capital head of a pillar or column

citizens men who were born in a city to parents who were citizens. A citizen had rights in their own city, which they would not have had in any other. Women could not be citizens.

city state a city and the land it controls around it

civilization a society of a period or place

column cylinder-shaped support for the roof of a building

debate formal discussion

democracy 'rule by the people' – this is when at least some ordinary people get to take part in running the country

geometry study of the shape of objects and how the shapes can be written down mathematically

gymnasium place where Greek men went to exercise in the open air

hoplites soldiers who fought on foot with spears and swords

orchestra the main central part of a theatre where the actors chanted, sang and danced

pankration an olympic event that was a combination of boxing and wrestling

Parthenon the largest temple on the Acropolis at Athens

phalanx solid body of men that formed an almost invincible wall of shields and bristling spears against attackers

philosopher person who thinks carefully about things and how they work

priest a person who works in a temple serving a god or goddess

ram sail straight into another ship in order to try and sink it

religious festival several days of religious ceremonies, usually held every year

sacrifice something given to a god or a goddess as a gift. If the sacrifice was a living thing then it would be killed before it was given.

slaves people who are owned by other, richer people. They can be bought and sold and are not free to leave. Slaves must do work for their owners.

trade a job, e.g. shoemaking is a trade

trireme Greek warship with three banks of oars, requiring 170 oarsmen and carrying a total of 200 men

Index

Titles in the *New Explore History* series include:

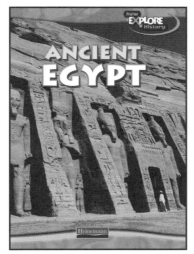

Hardback   0 431 07902 1

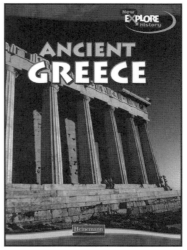

Hardback   0 431 07905 6

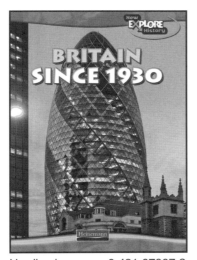

Hardback   0 431 07907 2

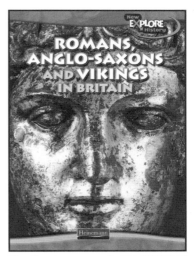

Hardback   0 431 07903 X

Hardback   0 431 07904 8

Hardback   0 431 07906 4

Find out about other titles from Heinemann Library on our website www.heinemann.co.uk/library